Backyard Animals
Bees
Edited by Heather C. Hudak

Weigl Publishers Inc.

Published by Weigl Publishers Inc.
350 5th Avenue, Suite 3304, PMB 6G
New York, NY 10118-0069
Website: www.weigl.com

Library of Congress Cataloging-in-Publication Data available upon request.
Fax 1-866-44-WEIGL for the attention of the Publishing Records department.

ISBN 978-1-60596-003-6 (hard cover)
ISBN 978-1-60596-009-8 (soft cover)

Printed in the United States of America
1 2 3 4 5 6 7 8 9 0 12 11 10 09 08

Editor Heather C. Hudak
Design Terry Paulhus

All of the Internet URLs given in the book were valid at the time of publication.
However, due to the dynamic nature of the Internet, some addresses may have
changed, or sites may have ceased to exist since publication. While the author
and publisher regret any inconvenience this may cause readers, no responsibility
for any such changes can be accepted by either the author or the publisher.

Photo Credits

Weigl acknowledges Getty Images as its primary image supplier for this title.

Every reasonable effort has been made to trace ownership and to obtain permission
to reprint copyright material. The publishers would be pleased to have any errors
or omissions brought to their attention so that they may be corrected in
subsequent printings.

Contents

Meet the Bee

Bees are insects. Insects are small animals that have an exoskeleton. The exoskeleton is a shell that protects the bee's body.

Bees live in almost all parts of the world. They can be found any place where flowers grow. This is because bees must eat **pollen** and **nectar** from flowers to survive. Many types of bees are social. They live in colonies, or groups, of 20,000 to 30,000 bees.

All bees have wings, **antennae**, and a tongue to help them find nectar and pollen. Bees help flowers **reproduce** by carrying their pollen from one flower to another. Flowers use this pollen to make seeds. Many types of bees make honey from the nectar they collect.

Many bees have stingers. They use these to protect themselves from **predators**.

The queen bee is an adult female who gives birth to all the bees in a colony.

All about Bees

Bees can be found in all parts of the world except for Antarctica. They come from a family of insects called *Apocrita*. This family includes wasps and ants. Bees are hairier than wasps and usually have rounder bodies.

There are nearly 20,000 **species** of bee. Bees range in size from 0.08 to 1.5 inches (2 to 38 millimeters) long. *Perdita minima* is one of the smallest types of bee. The largest bee is the *Megachile Pluto*.

Honeybees can fly up to 8.6 miles (14 kilometers) from their nest in search of food. They can fly at the speed of 15 miles (24 km) per hour.

Where Bees Live

Sweat bee

- Found in the United States, Canada, and Central America

Carpenter bee

- Live in the western United States and Mexico

Bumblebee

- Found in almost all northern parts of the world; most commonly found in the United States

Honeybee

- First came from Asia and the Middle East; live all over the world today

Bee History

Scientists are not sure how long bees have been on Earth. The oldest **fossils** of bees date back to more than 100 million years ago.

Bees developed from an ancient type of wasp that ate other kinds of insects. Many of these insects would eat pollen. Often, the wasps ate the pollen-covered insects. The wasps then began eating pollen as part of their food. Over time, these wasps became bees that feed on pollen.

Until the 1660s, the queen bee was known as the king. At this time, scientists learned that the biggest bee was female, not male.

Wasp

Bee

Sawfly

Ant

Bees, sawflies, wasps, and ants are from the Apocrita family. This family of insects has lived on Earth for many centuries.

Bee Habitat

Bees live mainly in places that are warm and sunny. This is because there are usually more flowers in places with a great deal of sunshine.

Bees live in many kinds of **habitats**. Some live in beehives. In nature, beehives are made out of **honeycomb** and wax. They often can be found in the hollows of trees or in caves. Human-made beehives are usually made out of wood. They are used to make honey.

Beehives have tightly packed cells that are made of wax. Some beehives have up to 100,000 bees living in them.

Orchid bees are brightly colored. This helps them to blend in with the orchids they feed on.

Bee Features

Bees have many special features. They use different body parts to help them find food, eat, fly, and protect themselves from predators.

ANTENNAE
Bees have two antennae that they use to smell flowers, which helps them know what kind of nectar they have found. Antennae also help bees feel objects.

EYES
Bees can see almost all colors, except for red. They can see some colors that humans cannot, such as shades of **ultraviolet**.

WINGS

Bees have two pairs of wings. The buzzing noise that bees make is the sound of their wings **vibrating**.

STINGER

Some bees have stingers. This helps protect them against threats, including other insects and animals. Bees only use their stinger if they are upset or angry.

What Do Bees Eat?

Bees eat nectar from flowers. They use their long tongue to suck the nectar out of the flowers. They turn the nectar into honey. Bees store the honey so that they can eat it during winter, when there are not enough flowers to feed on.

When bees land on flowers, the pollen sticks to their body. This pollen is carried back to the beehive. Bees use the pollen to feed their **larvae**. Energy from the pollen helps the larvae develop into bees.

Flowers come in all sorts of colors to attract bees. Just like bees have developed over time to carry pollen, flowers have developed to become brighter and more attractive to bees.

Humans, bears, badgers, and other animals eat the honey that bees make from nectar.

Bee Life Cycle

The life span of a bee depends on what role it has in the hive. The queen bee can live from two to five years. Drones are male bees that are used only for mating. They live between 40 and 50 days.

Eggs

The queen lays eggs to make sure her hive is filled with worker bees. A bee egg is about 0.04 inches (1.2 mm) long. The queen checks all the cells in the hive to find the cleanest and safest one before laying an egg inside. The queen can lay up to 1,900 eggs in one day.

Larvae

The eggs hatch into larvae after three days. The larvae look like grains of rice. For the next five days, larvae eat and grow. Nurse bees feed the larvae a mix of honey and pollen.

Worker bees are females. They live between one and four months. They do all of the work in the hive. Worker bees also help the queen and drones find food and mate.

Pupae

Larvae become **pupae** after nine days in the cell. The pupae start to develop all the features of a bee. They grow wings and legs, and hair appears on their body. Pupae do not eat for the entire time they are in their cells.

Adult

After 21 days, bees are fully grown and ready to start working for the hive. Worker bees do many jobs. These include cleaning out the cells where the queen lays her eggs, nursing the larvae, and building the beehive. The worker bees then help guard the hive until they become honey-collecting bees.

Encountering Bees

Bee farms and gardens with plenty of flowers are common places to see bees. During summer, bees are very active. This is because there are more flowers in bloom at this time.

Many bees sting when they are upset. However, bees will only sting if they are not left alone.

To prevent being stung by a bee, dress in long pants and a long-sleeved top when near a beehive. Wearing bright clothes will attract bees. If you are planning to spend time outdoors, wear white or pale colors. If you do get stung, remove the stinger, and apply ice to the area. Some people are **allergic** to bee stings. If you are allergic, you may need to seek help from a doctor.

Useful Websites

For more information on bees, visit
**www.sandiegozoo.org/
animalbytes/t-bee.html**.

Beekeepers wear a net and special clothing when they collect honey. This keeps them from being stung.

Myths and Legends

There are many myths and legends from all over the world about bees. Many of these stories are about bees being linked to different gods.

A Welsh legend says that a bee buzzing around a sleeping child means the child will have a happy life. This is because the Welsh thought bees were "messengers of god."

The Hindu gods Vishnu and Indra are often shown as bees in drawings and pictures. This is because bees are fast and carry honey, which is sweet.

Egyptians put bees in the tombs of their pharaohs, along with honey, so that the pharaohs could take bees with them to heaven.

The Egyptians had a god called Ra. They believed that Ra created bees from his own tears.

Jupiter and the Queen Bee

The Romans had many stories about bees being special creatures. One story is about how bees got their stingers. A queen bee collected all the fresh honey from her beehive. She took the honey up Mount Olympus to give to the god Jupiter as a gift. Jupiter was a very powerful god and was happy when he saw the fresh honey. He asked the queen bee to make any wish she wanted. The queen bee was very clever and decided to use her wish to help the rest of the bees. She asked Jupiter to give stingers to all bees so that they could protect themselves. Jupiter granted her wish, but he was angry that she wished for something so selfish. He added that if the bees used the stingers, they would die. This is why bees die after losing their stinger.

Frequently Asked Questions

Can there be more than one queen bee in a hive?

Answer: There is only one queen bee in a hive. The queen bee needs plenty of space to lay her eggs. Queen bees that are born in the hive fight each other until only one is left to rule the hive.

How far can bees fly?

Answer: An average worker bee can fly up to 8.5 miles (13.7 km) in one trip. The queen bee and drones do not fly nearly as much because they do not need to search for food.

Do bees dance?

Answer: All bees have their own dance that helps them communicate with each other. This is how one bee tells the others the best places to find nectar.

Puzzler

See if you can answer these questions about bees.

1. How do bees protect themselves?
2. How many queen bees are there in a hive?
3. What is the largest type of bee?
4. How old are the oldest bee fossils?
5. What do bees make from nectar?

Answers: 1. With stingers 2. One 3. Megachile Pluto 4. 100 million years 5. Honey

Find Out More

There are many more interesting facts to learn about bees. Look for these books at your library so you can learn more.

Hodge, Deborah, and Julian Mulock. *Bees*. Kids Can Press Limited, 2004.

Hubbell, Sue, and Sam Patthoff. *A Book of Bees: And How to Keep Them*. Houghton Mifflin Company, 1998.

Words to Know

allergic: to have a bad physical reaction to something

antennae: long, thin body parts that extend from an insect's head

fossils: the hardened remains of animals or plants that lived long ago

habitats: natural environments of living things

honeycomb: cells of wax made by bees

larvae: a stage in a bee's life when it eats to grow and has no physical features

nectar: liquid food from plants

pollen: a yellow powder produced by flowers

predators: animals that hunt other animals for food

pupae: a stage in a bee's life when it does not eat and develops its physical features

reproduce: to have offspring

species: animals or plants that share certain features

ultraviolet: light that is invisible to the human eye

vibrating: moving up and down or to and fro very quickly and repeatedly

Index